La Corbière

A play in one act

by

Anne Le Marquand Hartigan

CHISWICK BOOKS

LONDON

www.chiswickbooks.com

First published in 2016 by Chiswick Books
2 Prebend Gardens, Chiswick, London W4 1TW
email: info@chiswickbooks.com
website: www.chiswickbooks.com

La Corbière copyright © Anne Le Marquand Hartigan 1989.
Anne Le Marquand Hartigan is hereby identified as author of this play in accordance with section 77 of the Copyright, Designs and Patents Act 1988. The author has asserted her moral rights.

All rights whatsoever in this play are strictly reserved and application for performance etc. should be made before commencement of rehearsal to email: rights@annehartigan.ie. No performance may be given unless a licence has been obtained, and no alterations may be made in the title or the text of the play without the author's prior written consent.

This book is sold subject to the condition that it shall not by way of trade or otherwise be circulated without the publisher's consent in any form of binding or cover or circulated electronically other than that in which it is published and without a similar condition including this condition being imposed on any subsequent purchaser.

British Library Cataloguing in Publication Data. A catalogue record for this book is available from the British Library.

This is a work of fiction. Names, characters, places and incidents either are products of the author's imagination or are used fictitiously. Any resemblance to actual events or locales or persons, living or dead, is entirely coincidental.

ISBN: 978-0-9928692-6-7

Cover image from a painting by Anne Le Marquand Hartigan.

Also by the author

Plays

Beds, *Chiswick Books, 2016*
I Do Like to be Beside the Seaside, *Chiswick Books, 2016*
Jersey Lilies, *Chiswick Books, 2016*
Three Short Plays, *Chiswick Books, 2016*
The Secret Game, *Chiswick Books, 2014*

Poetry

Unsweet Dreams, *Salmon Poetry, 2011*
To Keep The Light Burning, *Salmon Poetry, 2008*
Nourishment, *Salmon Poetry, 2005*
Immortal Sins, *Salmon Poetry, 1995*
Now is a Moveable Feast, *Salmon Poetry, 1991*
Return Single, *Beaver Row Press, 1986*
Long Tongue, *Beaver Row Press, 1982*

Prose

Clearing the Space, *Salmon Poetry, 1996*

To Cathy Leeney with thanks for all her creative input.

La Corbière was first produced by Moveable Feast Theatre Company as part of the Dublin Theatre Festival at the Project Arts Centre in October 1989 with the following cast:

MARIE-CLAIRE	Eithne Dempsey
ANGÉLIQUE	Virginia Cole
DÉSIRÉE	Joy Forsythe
CÉLESTE	Clodagh O'Donoghue
KURT	Joe Hanley
KLAUS	Declan Walsh
MAN ON THE PHONE	Joe Hanley
SAILOR ONE	Joe Hanley
SAILOR TWO	Declan Walsh
Director	Cathy Leeney
Designers	Pauline Donnelly and Dominic Hartigan
Lighting	Paul O'Neill
Costumes	Máire Hearty, Máire O'Higgins and Kirsty McGhie
Production Manager	Dominic Hartigan

Characters

MARIE-CLAIRE	*Survivor of the wreck*
ANGÉLIQUE	*Drowned woman*
DÉSIRÉE	*Drowned woman*
CÉLESTE	*Drowned woman*
KURT	*Young Nazi soldier*
KLAUS	*Young Nazi soldier*
MAN ON THE PHONE	
SAILOR ONE	*On the wrecked boat*
SAILOR TWO	*On the wrecked boat*

Note

The island of Jersey in the Channel Islands was occupied
by the Nazis during the Second World War. The Nazis
imported a boatload of French prostitutes from Normandy
in 1941 for the entertainment of the troops. They were
housed at the Hotel Victor Hugo. There were about forty of
them, none of them young. The project was not a success
and the whores were shipped off again in a Dutch coaster.
Fog came down and the coaster struck rocks and sank
in a matter of minutes with the loss of all on board. The
ship sank on the fiercely rocky coast near La Corbière
lighthouse. The women's bodies were seen floating in the
sea for days, sometimes alone and sometimes in clusters,
their long peroxide hair floating out on the waves.

Act One

Scene One

The Wreck

Foghorn, sea sounds. The women are being returned to France on a coaster which is wrecked on the rocks at La Corbière by a terrible storm.

DÉSIRÉE

> Where am I? I can't see.

MARIE-CLAIRE

> Give me your hand.

DÉSIRÉE

> What hand? Is that you?

MARIE-CLAIRE

> I don't know. I can't see.

DÉSIRÉE

> I'm here. Touch me. Where are you for God's sake?

MARIE-CLAIRE

>All my life it has been like this.

DÉSIRÉE

>This is stupid. I can't find you.

MARIE-CLAIRE

>All my life, in fog just like this. Dumb.

DÉSIRÉE

>I keep expecting to see the light. La Corbière light.

MAN ON THE PHONE

>*Receiving Morse code.*
>
>Visibility now nil at La Corbière.

DÉSIRÉE

>*Sings*
>
>Me and my dog, were lost in the fog, will some kind gentleman see me home?

ANGÉLIQUE

>Here we are leaving this bloody island at last, stuck in pea soup. Mother of God.

CÉLESTE

>You can always swim for it.

DÉSIRÉE

> When things got really bad at home, my brother and I would swim to the island. We thought nothing of it. Was it a mile or more? I can't even remember.
>
> *Sound of Morse code.*

MAN ON THE PHONE

> *Receiving Morse code message.*
>
> Distress. Ship in distress. Ship in distress off La Corbière.

CÉLESTE

> I can't see. Where are you Marie-Claire?

MARIE-CLAIRE

> Here. I'm here.

DÉSIRÉE

> Where's here?

CÉLESTE

> How the fuck does she know?

ANGÉLIQUE

> Under this huge tide, rows of rocks ready to eat you. Teeth.
>
> *Sound of Morse code.*

LA CORBIÈRE

MAN ON THE PHONE

> Warning to all shipping. Dense fog reported from La Corbière.

CÉLESTE

> Friendly!

ANGELIQUE

> Hope this captain knows what he's at.

CÉLESTE

> I doubt it.

MARIE-CLAIRE

> Where are you?

CÉLESTE

> I don't know. I can't see. Touch me.

MARIE-CLAIRE

> Where are you? I can't hear.
>
> *Sound of Morse code.*

MAN ON THE PHONE

> Warning. Warning to all shipping. Warning. Dense fog reported from La Corbière.

DÉSIRÉE

> Where are you?
>
> *The wreck takes place. Sea sounds. Foghorn.*

S.O.S. in Morse code. Voices of men as CAPTAIN, SAILORS, shout. All the women drown except MARIE-CLAIRE.

DÉSIRÉE

>Where are you?

CÉLESTE

>I can't swim.

ANGÉLIQUE

>I can't swim.

CÉLESTE

>Where are you?

MARIE-CLAIRE

>Where are the boats?

MAN ON THE PHONE

>A coaster has hit rocks off La Corbière. Believe all hands have been lost.

CÉLESTE

>I can't swim.

DÉSIRÉE

>Hold on.

ANGÉLIQUE

>Marie-Claire?

DÉSIRÉE

    Hold on.

MAN ON THE PHONE

    Hold on. I can't hear. Hold on.

CÉLESTE

    Don't leave me.

DÉSIRÉE

    Where am I?

CÉLESTE

    I can't swim.

MARIE-CLAIRE

    Hold. Hold. Hold.

SAILORS

    Hold on. Hold on. Hold on. Jump. Hold that. Jump.

MAN ON THE PHONE

    The lines are down. The lines are out. The lines are bad.

SAILOR

    Throw a line. Throw, throw a line, throw…

MARIE-CLAIRE

    Hold on.

DÉSIRÉE

    Hold on.

SAILOR

    A line.

MAN ON THE PHONE

    The lines are bad. Hold. Wait. Hold the line…

SAILOR

    Throw a line. Quick, quick.

SAILOR

    Your hand, give me your hand.

SAILOR ONE

    Jump. Jump away from the ship.

MARIE-CLAIRE

    Jump. Jump.

ANGÉLIQUE

    Hold out your hand. Where is your hand?

DÉSIRÉE

    Your hand, your hand, where is your hand?

CÉLESTE

    Help me.

MAN ON THE PHONE

    I can't hear. I can't hear you.

CÉLESTE

>Oh help me.

MAN ON THE PHONE

>Hold.

MARIE-CLAIRE

>Hold on to me.

DÉSIRÉE

>Hold here.

MAN ON THE PHONE

>Hold on. I can't hear, the conditions are bad, hold on a minute.

CÉLESTE

>Hold on. Here, here, here.

ANGÉLIQUE

>Give it to me.

CÉLESTE

>For God's sake, I can't swim.

ANGÉLIQUE

>For God's sake, for God's sake.

MARIE-CLAIRE

>Where are you? Where? I can't see you.

DÉSIRÉE

>Where have you gone?

CÉLESTE

>I'm gone. I can't see. I can't hold on.

DÉSIRÉE

>Can't, I can't, can't.

ANGÉLIQUE

>Can't hold.

MARIE-CLAIRE

>Jump.

CÉLESTE

>I can't.

MARIE-CLAIRE

>You can.

ANGÉLIQUE

>I can't.

MARIE-CLAIRE

>Jump. You can. You can. Do it. Do it.
>
>*The women are in the water.*

DÉSIRÉE

>Throw a line.

MARIE-CLAIRE

>Throw a line. Where are you? Hang on.

DÉSIRÉE

>Where are you? Where are you?

CÉLESTE

>I can't see you.

ANGÉLIQUE

>I can't swim. Oh my God.

DÉSIRÉE

>I can't touch you.

ANGÉLIQUE

>I can't keep up. Mother of God. Holy Mother.

MARIE-CLAIRE

>Angélique, Désirée, Céleste…?

ANGÉLIQUE

>Where is she? She's gone.

DÉSIRÉE

>She's gone.

CÉLESTE

>I'm going.

ANGÉLIQUE

>I can't feel, I can't keep up, God help me.

MARIE-CLAIRE

>Where are you, Désirée, Désirée, Désirée?

CÉLESTE

>I can't, I can't swim, I can't hold on.

MAN ON THE PHONE

>I can't hear. Nothing. Nothing. I can hear nothing.

DÉSIRÉE

>There is nothing to hold, nothing.

CÉLESTE

>Help.

ANGÉLIQUE

>Help.

CÉLESTE

>Help.

ANGÉLIQUE

>Don't leave me, don't leave me, I can't.

DÉSIRÉE

>Nothing, nothing.

ALL

>Whooorrre.
>
>*Silence.*

Scene Two

Marie-Claire Mourns for Those Drowned

La Corbière lighthouse sweeps its light across the stage and audience: light/dark, light/dark. Sea sounds. Gull cry.

MARIE-CLAIRE
    Corbière, Corbière, Corbière

DÉSIRÉE
    air

MARIE-CLAIRE
    hair

DÉSIRÉE
    air

MARIE-CLAIRE
    hair Corbière, Corbière, Corbière

MAN ON THE PHONE
    requiem aeternam dona eis, Domine

MARIE-CLAIRE
    Corbière

DÉSIRÉE
> Corpus

MARIE-CLAIRE
> Corbière

DÉSIRÉE
> Christi

MARIE-CLAIRE   KLAUS
> Corbière   whore

DÉSIRÉE   KURT
> Corpus   whore

MARIE-CLAIRE   KLAUS
> Corbière   whore

DÉSIRÉE   KURT
> Christi   whore

MAN ON THE PHONE   KLAUS
> Requiem aeternam   whore
> dona eis, Domine

MARIE-CLAIRE   KURT
> Corbière   whore

DÉSIRÉE   KLAUS
> air air air   whore

MARIE-CLAIRE

    hair hair hair

KURT

    whore

MAN ON THE PHONE

    Requiem aerternam

    dona eis, Domine

KLAUS

    whore

KURT

    lot

KLAUS

    their lot

MAN ON THE PHONE

    got their lot

KURT

    deserved

KLAUS

    their lot

KURT

    harlot harlot

KLAUS

    harlot harlot

MARIE-CLAIRE:

    Roars.

    Whore. Rise up ye strong whores. Rise.

DÉSIRÉE

    whore

CÉLESTE

    whore

MARIE-CLAIRE

    whore

ANGELIQUE

    whore

CÉLESTE

    whore

DÉSIRÉE

    whore

MARIE-CLAIRE

    whore

DÉSIRÉE

    whore

CÉLESTE

    whore

KURT

    har lot har lot har lot

KLAUS

    har lot har lot har lot

MARIE-CLAIRE

>*Quietly.*
>
>Rise up ye strong whores. Sisters rise up, strong. Strong sisters. Wronged sisters. I will weep for thee, mourn for thee, cry for thee. In the strong salt sea will long for thee, sea sister, water sister, we will howl for thee, banshee for thee, weep for thee as the salt sea seep for thee.
>
>*Following words uttered as sea sounds and can be repeated and interwoven.*

SAILOR ONE

>slop

SAILOR TWO

>clop, clop

SAILOR ONE

>flop smack lack back

SAILOR TWO

>the rock teeth the rock teeth, the teeth

SAILOR ONE

>the grate grind grit growl, the suck back

SAILOR TWO

>shoal grawl, hiss hawl hisshawl, hisshawl

SAILOR ONE

    gravel

SAILOR TWO

    drawl

SAILOR ONE

    drawldown suckback back

ALL

    whhoooorrre

    Sea sounds end. Silence.

KLAUS

    straight

KURT

    flat

KLAUS

    empty

KURT

    iron

KLAUS

    terrible as tin

KURT

    a lining fallen from the grey sky

KLAUS

>nothing

KURT

>all barbarities buried, the rock teeth and ripped flesh

KLAUS

>nothing

KURT

>there is nothing

KLAUS

>nothing but the sea

DÉSIRÉE

>our tears are salt

CÉLESTE

>and the sea

DÉSIRÉE

>the sea salt

CÉLESTE

>and our tears

ANGÉLIQUE

>weep

CÉLESTE

    weeping the sea salt

ANGÉLIQUE

    and our tears

CÉLESTE

    weeping the salt

ANGÉLIQUE

    from the sea

DÉSIRÉE

    salt salt salt

    Building up to:

ALL WOMEN

    assault!

MARIE-CLAIRE

    Low growl

    assault

KURT

    rape

MARIE-CLAIRE

    salt

KURT

    rape

MARIE-CLAIRE

> sea, seasalt

KURT

> rapesalt

MARIE-CLAIRE

> rapesalt weep

DÉSIRÉE

> asleep

ANGÉLIQUE

> dead

CÉLESTE

> beat beat

KURT

> beat dead

MARIE-CLAIRE

> deadbeat

KURT

> beatdead

MARIE-CLAIRE

> deadbeat

KURT

> beatdead beatdead beatdead

MARIE-CLAIRE
> salt salt salt salt salt

DÉSIRÉE
> bereft

CÉLESTE
> bereft

ANGÉLIQUE
> bereft.

Scene Three

The Arrival

Bright, sunny; gentle sound of a zephyr. ALL sing 'A Boatload of Whores' to a jaunty tune.

ALL

>A boatload of whores
>
>From over the sea
>
>One fine day, one fine day,
>
>A boatload of whores
>
>From over the sea
>
>One fine day in the morning.
>
>
>Oh they were happy
>
>As happy could be
>
>One fine day, one fine day,
>
>Oh they were merry
>
>As they could be
>
>One fine day in the morning.

You'll come to Jersey

And you'll have fun

One fine day, one fine day,

MEN

Just move along

At the butt of my gun

One fine day in the morning.

ALL

Leave your home

And leave your child

One fine day, one fine day,

The weather there

Is always mild,

One fine day in the morning.

Who cares if your mother

Is bombed while you're gone?

One fine day, one fine day,

Whores like you/us

Are not worth a song,

One fine day in the morning.

Whores like you/us

Are lucky to live

One fine day, one fine day,

Who cares if this boat

Is only a sieve?

One fine day in the morning.

Repeat first verse.

Sudden blackout. The two Nazis shine torches at the women's faces. One woman shines a torch at the men's boots and at her own and the other women's feet. The torches are blacked out apart from a cross through which the light shines. Otherwise blackout.

CÉLESTE

    We've arrived.

ANGÉLIQUE

    I hate journeys.

DÉSIRÉE

    I hate arriving.

MARIE-CLAIRE

    We've got here.

DÉSIRÉE

> At least we didn't hit a mine.

CÉLESTE

> *Sarcastic.*
>
> We are so lucky, lucky little us, off on our hols.
> Oh goody.

MARIE-CLAIRE

> Belt up.

CÉLESTE

> Vive la France. I'm so happy.

MARIE-CLAIRE

> I'll shut your mouth if you don't belt up.

KLAUS

> Silence.

KURT

> Pick up your bags.

KLAUS

> Have your papers ready.

KURT

> Move along.

KLAUS

> Move. You may not speak to anyone.

CÉLESTE

> I'd kill for a fag.

DÉSIRÉE

> It's the end of the journey.

MARIE-CLAIRE

> You mean it's the beginning.

ANGÉLIQUE	MARIE-CLAIRE
What did I forget?	What did I remember?

CÉLESTE

> Have you a fag, sonny?

KLAUS

> Silence.

KURT

> You may not speak.

KLAUS

> You will obey orders. There will be silence.

KURT

> You may not show any light whatsoever.

CÉLESTE

> They don't understand French.

MARIE-CLAIRE

>Little shits.

ANGÉLIQUE

>I'm frightened.

DÉSIRÉE

>End of the journey.

MARIE-CLAIRE

>It's only the beginning.

ANGÉLIQUE

>It's better to travel than to arrive.

DÉSIRÉE

>It was better on the journey, just travelling.

MARIE-CLAIRE

>If we'd struck a mine that would have been that.

DÉSIRÉE

>I've got stomach cramps.

CÉLESTE

>I was seasick.

MARIE-CLAIRE

>Stop complaining.

ANGÉLIQUE

>My feet are killing me.

MARIE-CLAIRE

>Will I see her again?

CÉLESTE

>Did we turn off the gas?

DÉSIRÉE

>My head is throbbing.

ANGÉLIQUE

>Will she mind him properly?

DÉSIRÉE

>Will he be there when I get home? Will I get home?

ANGÉLIQUE

>Hail Mary full of grace, the Lord is with thee.

KLAUS

>Name, date of birth, nationality?

CÉLESTE

>Céleste Vidal, thirty-five, born Lyon, France.

KLAUS

>Hey, look at this one, says she's thirty–five, forty if she's a day, French whore! Looks like a Jewish whore to me.

KURT

> Very like a Jewish whore, an old bag of a Jewish whore.

KLAUS

> Make a note of that one, something will have to be done about that one.

KURT

> She'll be for the chop.
>
> *They laugh.*

MARIE-CLAIRE

> Don't mind them. They're only whipper-snappers.

DÉSIRÉE

> They took my sister.

CÉLESTE

> They took my brother.

ANGÉLIQUE

> This suitcase is deadly. My veins are aching.

DÉSIRÉE

> I've got my period.

CÉLESTE

> Will they be bombed? They shot the dog.

DÉSIRÉE

>Have you got an aspirin?

CÉLESTE

>I hate the sea.

ANGÉLIQUE

>I've broken a nail.

MARIE-CLAIRE

>Listen you girls, if they haven't got nylons on this island I'm hopping on the next boat home.
>
>*Laughs.*

KURT

>Silence.

KLAUS

>You will proceed to exit 'Y' immediately. Take with you only what you carry. You must not speak.

KURT

>You will show no light whatsoever. It is forbidden to smoke.
>
>*Exeunt; two torchlights shining on women's feet. Men sing or hum 'A Boatload of Whores.'*

Scene Four

The Whores on the Island, Their Routine Walk.

Men speak quietly, often rhythmically as water slopping on rocks, under and through the women. Each woman steps forward as she says her name, the light shines on her face as she does so.

KURT
>Each day a crocodile of women.

ANGÉLIQUE	KURT
Angélique Duval	slop clop slop
CÉLESTE	KLAUS
Céleste Vidal	slit slut slit
MARIE-CLAIRE	KURT
Marie-Claire Depret	slop clop slop
DÉSIRÉE	KLAUS
Désirée Montard	slit slut slit

KURT, KLAUS
>cochon merde putain

CÉLESTE
    Monique Cerdan

KLAUS
    slit slut slit

MARIE-CLAIRE
    Zoë Barrier

KURT
    clop slop clop

CÉLESTE
    Yvonne Préjean

KLAUS
    slut slit slut

DÉSIRÉE
    Yves Coutet

KURT
    slop clop slop

ANGÉLIQUE
    Irma Dubas

KLAUS
    slit slut slit

CÉLESTE
    Elis Meurisse

KURT
    slop clop slop

MARIE-CLAIRE
    Francine Dumont

KLAUS
    slut slit slut

CÉLESTE
    Valérie Robert

KURT
    slop clop slop

DÉSIRÉE
    Véronique Caron

KLAUS
    slit slut slit

ANGÉLIQUE
    Hélène Leduc

KURT
    clop slop clop

KURT
    slit cunt fuck merde cochon putain

KLAUS

    fuck cunt slit merde cochon putain

KURT

    Each day a crocodile of girls. Two by two, in pairs, docile, captured.

CÉLESTE

    Marie-Claude

MARIE-CLAIRE

    Marie-Thérèse

KURT

    White veils? Throwing petals?

CÉLESTE

    Marie-Claire

DÉSIRÉE

    Marianne

KURT

    Through the flowering hedgerows, pale voices singing.

ANGÉLIQUE

    Marie-Rose

CÉLESTE

    Marie-Jeanne

KURT

>Herded, driven.

KLAUS

>Schoolgirls?

KURT

>Corpus Christi procession?

CÉLESTE

>Notre Dame, Notre Dame.

KLAUS

>Re-treads.

KURT

>Old sows, by the bare trees, in bright sun, two by two they snake the roads.

KLAUS

>Raddled, old.

KURT

>Under high hedges, heavy with summer.

DÉSIRÉE

>Désirée

CÉLESTE

>Céleste

ANGÉLIQUE
> Angélique

DÉSIRÉE
> Désirée

CÉLESTE
> Céleste

ANGÉLIQUE
> Angélique.

Scene Five

The Women's Dreams

Song: A lullaby is sung in the background to engender a peaceful, soft, gentle atmosphere.

CÉLESTE

>*As if dreaming about her wedding.*
>
>I, Céleste, take thee, Armand, to be my wedded husband, to have and hold from this day forward, for better, for worse, for richer, for poorer, in sickness and in health, till death do us part, and thereto I plight thee my troth.
>
>With this ring I thee wed, this gold and silver I thee give, with my body I thee worship, and with all my worldly goods I thee endow.
>
>*The following words float as if blown on the wind by the sea, as if rising up from the unconscious, in a dream.*

ANGÉLIQUE

>come home   mother

DÉSIRÉE

    my child's face   good

CÉLESTE

    sweet

DÉSIRÉE

    clean

ANGÉLIQUE

    bread   come home

CÉLESTE

    bed   sheet-white

ANGÉLIQUE

    come home   mother

CÉLESTE

    now

ANGÉLIQUE

    found

CÉLESTE

    safe

DÉSIRÉE, ANGÉLIQUE

    clean

ANGÉLIQUE

    safe   bread

CÉLESTE

>found

DÉSIRÉE

>soft warm

ANGÉLIQUE

>come home

DÉSIRÉE, ANGÉLIQUE

>mother

DÉSIRÉE

>baby's pink

CÉLESTE

>sweet

ANGÉLIQUE

>home mother

CÉLESTE

>soft

DÉSIRÉE

>good baby   warm

ANGÉLIQUE

>when?   when?   now

CÉLESTE

>safe

CÉLESTE, DÉSIRÉE
> always together

ANGÉLIQUE
> warm bread

DÉSIRÉE
> white   now

ANGÉLIQUE
> food

DÉSIRÉE
> warm cosy   mother

ANGÉLIQUE
> sister

DÉSIRÉE
> child

CÉLESTE
> gently

DÉSIRÉE
> good

CÉLESTE
> holy

ANGÉLIQUE
> now gently

LA CORBIÈRE

CÉLESTE

 never

DÉSIRÉE

 soft

ANGÉLIQUE

 always

DÉSIRÉE

 good

ANGÉLIQUE

 always

CÉLESTE, ANGÉLIQUE

 always always good

DÉSIRÉE

 always

CÉLESTE, ANGÉLIQUE, DÉSIRÉE

 always

CÉLESTE

 all

DÉSIRÉE

 ways

ANGÉLIQUE

 all

CÉLESTE

> ways

ANGÉLIQUE

> all

CÉLESTE

> ways

CÉLESTE, DÉSIRÉE

> ways ways ways ways

CÉLESTE

> apart

ANGÉLIQUE

> ways apart

CÉLESTE

> us do part

ANGÉLIQUE

> apart

DÉSIRÉE

> gap

CÉLESTE

> broken
>
> *KLAUS rapes DÉSIRÉE. KURT is also involved.*

Women frightened, speak quietly under rape scene.

DÉSIRÉE	**MARIE-CLAIRE**
broken open	gather
KLAUS	**CÉLESTE**
now	keep
MARIE-CLAIRE	**ANGÉLIQUE**
alert	stay
DÉSIRÉE	**MARIE-CLAIRE**
not	hold
MARIE-CLAIRE	**ANGÉLIQUE**
alert	belong
DÉSIRÉE	**CÉLESTE**
not now please	trust
stop no	
DÉSIRÉE	**ANGÉLIQUE**
not that	trust
KURT	**MARIE-CLAIRE**
here	collect
	hoard hold
	stay be long
	long

DÉSIRÉE   MARIE-CLAIRE
    don't   please stop   stay keep trust
    don't   no   not that   be   long
    Mother   said   trust
    please don't
    no   not
    I don't   like this

KLAUS   ANGÉLIQUE
    like this   always

DÉSIRÉE   CÉLESTE
    like this   all ways

KLAUS   MARIE-CLAIRE
    like this   always

DÉSIRÉE   CÉLESTE
    like this   trust

KLAUS   ANGÉLIQUE
    like this   keep

DÉSIRÉE   MARIE-CLAIRE
    like this   touch

KLAUS   CÉLESTE
    like this   be long
    like this

Scene Six

Cabaret in Hotel Victor Hugo

Can be performed without physical contact. Men shouting the words and women miming their pain.

Dance music.

KLAUS

    tickle

    All women giggle.

KURT

    slap

    All women laugh/weep.

KLAUS

    punch

    All women.weep/cry out/protest

KLAUS

    tickle

    All women giggle.

KURT

    slap

All women laugh/weep.

KLAUS

punch

All women.weep/cry out/protest

KLAUS

tickle

All women giggle.

KURT

slap

All women laugh/weep.

KLAUS

punch

All women.weep/cry out/protest

This is repeated, getting faster and faster:

KLAUS

punch

KURT

punch

KLAUS

punch

KURT

punch

KLAUS

>	punch

KURT

>	punch

KLAUS

>	punch

>	*Silence.*

MARIE-CLAIRE

>	Rise up from the bottom of the sea. Rise up from the bottom of their minds. Rise up. Push down the sea. Rise. Shout out so loud that the world will burst. From the bottom of the sea, the world will burst.

>	*Sounds of jackboots, bursts of machine-gun fire. KURT and KLAUS link arms and dance and sing. MARIE-CLAIRE, DÉSIRÉE, CÉLESTE link arms and dance and sing. Faces masked in stockings, Soldiers stick out their tongues. Two groups confront each other.*

Scene Seven

The Healing Sea

Sea sounds. La Corbière light.

DÉSIRÉE

     shore

CÉLESTE

     whore

DÉSIRÉE

     shore

CÉLESTE

     whore

ANGÉLIQUE

     swell

DÉSIRÉE

     shore

CÉLESTE

     whore

ANGÉLIQUE

     drawl

DÉSIRÉE

> sea shore seashore

CÉLESTE

> whore

ANGÉLIQUE

> child

CÉLESTE

> sand

CÉLESTE

> sea

DÉSIRÉE

> sea sea sea

CÉLESTE

> stone

DÉSIRÉE

> rock

CÉLESTE

> sea

ANGÉLIQUE

> swellchild swell with child

CÉLESTE

> swell with sea

DÉSIRÉE

> swell with stone

CÉLESTE

> swell with sea

DÉSIRÉE

> swell with stone

MARIE-CLAIRE

> There is no answer but stone.

Scene Eight

Flashback to the Wreck

They are in fog. Fog horn, La Corbière light.

DÉSIRÉE

> Where am I? I can't see.

MARIE-CLAIRE

> Give me your hand.

DÉSIRÉE

> What hand? Is that you?

MARIE-CLAIRE

> I don't know. I can't see.

DÉSIRÉE

> I'm here. Touch me.

MARIE-CLAIRE

> Where are you?

DÉSIRÉE

> Where are you?

KURT

> The sea lies flat as tin.

KLAUS

> Flat as lies told down the black telephone receiver.

KURT

> The sea lies flatter than the earth, its mouth shut tight on the night sky. The sky cannot penetrate and the clouds blot out the moon. An ink stain on grey.

MAN ON THE PHONE

> Nothing.

KURT

> Nowhere. This is not.

MAN ON THE PHONE

> Negative. Finished. Silence.

KURT

> No gull cry. No sea sound.

MARIE-CLAIRE

> *Shouts.*
>
> There is no answer but stone.

Scene Nine

The Aftermath of the Wreck

Alternatively, this scene could be performed by MARIE-CLAIRE alone.

MARIE-CLAIRE

> *Walks as if on the seashore and coming across body parts of the women in the sand.*
>
> sand sand sand sand sand sand sand sand sand sand sand sand sand sand sand sand sand sand

CÉLESTE

> foot

MARIE-CLAIRE

> sand sand sand sand sand sand

CÉLESTE

> love

MARIE-CLAIRE

> sand sand sand

CÉLESTE

> breast

MARIE-CLAIRE

    sand sand sand sand sand sand sand sand

CÉLESTE

    belly

MARIE-CLAIRE

    sand sand sand sand sand sand sand sand

CÉLESTE

    cunt

MARIE-CLAIRE

    sand sand sand sand sand

CÉLESTE

    love

MARIE-CLAIRE

    sand sand sand sand sand sand sand sand sand
    sand sand

CÉLESTE

    shit

MARIE-CLAIRE

    sand

CÉLESTE

    rock

MARIE-CLAIRE

    sand

CÉLESTE

    rock

MARIE-CLAIRE

    sand

CÉLESTE

    rock

MARIE-CLAIRE

    sand

CÉLESTE

    slit rock crunch

MARIE-CLAIRE

    sand

CÉLESTE

    rock

MARIE-CLAIRE

    sand sand sand sand sand sand sand sand sand

CÉLESTE

    rockabye

MARIE-CLAIRE

    sand sand

CÉLESTE
> rock

MARIE-CLAIRE
> sand

CÉLESTE
> a-bye

MARIE-CLAIRE
> sand

CÉLESTE
> baby

MARIE-CLAIRE
> sand sand sand

CÉLESTE
> breast

MARIE-CLAIRE
> sand sand

CÉLESTE
> baby

MARIE-CLAIRE
> sand sand sand sand

CÉLESTE
> slit rock hand breast foot belly thigh flesh smell

rot gut rot

MARIE-CLAIRE

sand sand sand sand sand sand sand sand sand
sand sand sand sand

CÉLESTE

bone

MARIE-CLAIRE

sand sand

CÉLESTE

finger

MARIE-CLAIRE

sand

CÉLESTE

mouth

MARIE-CLAIRE

sand sand sand

CÉLESTE

lips

MARIE-CLAIRE

sand

CÉLESTE

smell

MARIE-CLAIRE

    sand

CÉLESTE

    taste

MARIE-CLAIRE

    sand sand

CÉLESTE

    dry

MARIE-CLAIRE

    sand sand sand

CÉLESTE

    wind

MARIE-CLAIRE

    sand sand

CÉLESTE

    cold dry cold dry

MARIE-CLAIRE

    sand sand sand sand sand

CÉLESTE

    cold wet wild cold dry baby breast foot mouth
    lips breast belly cunt love cunt breast lips mouth
    cold

Silence.

CÉLESTE

> *Utters as a drawn-out sigh:*
>
> dry

MARIE-CLAIRE

> sand

CÉLESTE

> bone   dead breast

MARIE-CLAIRE

> sand sand

CÉLESTE

> breast rot blue mould gut sand

MARIE-CLAIRE

> sand sand sand sand sand sand sand sand sand
> sand sand sand sand sand sand sand sand sand
> sand sand sand sand sand sand sand san sa s s s s
>
> s s s s s s
>
> *Silence.*

KURT

> The iron lid is on. The steel grey lid on the sea.
> Bolted down with rust.

KLAUS

> The sea is nailed to the shore, the moon at last is powerless.

KURT

> Nailed down. It cannot scream or flap.

KLAUS

> The last paper bag, blown.

KURT

> The last bottle sucks in its sides. The last black salted shoe loses a sole.

KLAUS

> night

KURT

> over

KLAUS

> finished

ANGÉLIQUE, CÉLESTE, DÉSIRÉE

> taboo taboo taboo

MARIE-CLAIRE

> The sea is bolted down, racked, drawn tight in a rictus smile, under this grey teeth of waves, they are buried.

KURT

>   They are finished.

KLAUS

>   They are scrubbed out.

MAN ON THE PHONE

>   Not known at this address.

MARIE-CLAIRE

>   This watery arbour, this stiff sea where the rock teeth lie, in unison, chorus.

MAN ON THE PHONE

>   Dateline.

Scene Ten

The Drowned Whores' Picnic

The dead women have a picnic under the sea.

DÉSIRÉE

    ripped

CÉLESTE

    eaten

DÉSIRÉE

    digested

CÉLESTE

    afloat in a shark's belly

DÉSIRÉE

    the eyeballs float apart

CÉLESTE

    the peroxide hair slimed

ANGÉLIQUE

    teeth and nose bridges litter the floorbed

CÉLESTE

    your seabed

DÉSIRÉE

> your last bed

CÉLESTE

> what the fuck

DÉSIRÉE

> who the fuck, we were the fucking professionals
> of fuck

CÉLESTE, DÉSIRÉE

> fish fuck!

ANGÉLIQUE

> your lovers

DÉSIRÉE

> your time-machines, your nothings, your holes

ANGÉLIQUE

> your forgetting

CÉLESTE

> your guiltholder

DÉSIRÉE

> your silences

CÉLESTE

> your dirt, your rubbish

DÉSIRÉE

> your hate, your violence, your punchball

ANGÉLIQUE

> your face, your mother

DÉSIRÉE

> your enemy

CÉLESTE

> your lies

ANGÉLIQUE

> your memory

DÉSIRÉE

> your toilet

CÉLESTE

> your headache

ANGÉLIQUE

> your madness

CÉLESTE

> your money, yours

ANGÉLIQUE

> your expense account, your throw-away

CÉLESTE

> your useless

DÉSIRÉE

> your dustbin, your disposable

CÉLESTE

> your waste

ANGÉLIQUE

> possessed

CÉLESTE

> owned for an hour

DÉSIRÉE

> bought

CÉLESTE

> sold

DÉSIRÉE

> less than cattle

ANGÉLIQUE

> herded

MARIE-CLAIRE

> Rise up ye strong whores. Sisters, rise up.
> Strong. Strong sisters. Wronged sisters.

ALL WOMEN

> *Roar.*
>
> whhooorre

Scene Eleven

Marie-Claire Laments the Drowned Whores

Abandoned, no one comes to take them from the sea.

MARIE-CLAIRE

    Corbière Corbière Corbière

DÉSIRÉE

    hair hair hair hair hair hair

MARIE-CLAIRE

    Corbière

DÉSIRÉE

    air

MARIE-CLAIRE

    Corbière

KURT

    lot

KLAUS

    their lot

KURT

    got their lot

KLAUS

>deserved

KURT

>their lot

KLAUS

>harlot harlot

ALL WOMEN

>rock and flow

MARIE-CLAIRE

>In clusters your bodies dance. Together you're flowers. Yellow hair spread on the sea's time.

ALL WOMEN

>rock and flow

MARIE-CLAIRE

>For a time you rest on the sea; balanced over rock cavities.

ALL WOMEN

>No one is coming.

MARIE-CLAIRE

>No one is coming with arms to dip. No strong arms to dip down you out from the sea's terror. No one. No white arms over the boat's side, to

reach over the edge. No one searching. No eyes eager as searchlights, as La Corbière light sweeps its arc over the storm. No one will lay you out in a quiet room. No one will light a candle at your head and feet. There will be no prayers. No one will push their boat out to take your bodies back to earth. You bob your last dance on the sea's foam. Flotsam. Rock and flow. Spread-eagled on the indifferent sea.

No chrism to anoint your brow. No incense around a coffin of wood. No name in the newspaper, no name. Sorrow is a lost word. There are no tears. Can the salt sea weep? Only a harsh gull's cry.

Silence.

Afterword

When writing a play I find I move from a visual image, whereas, with the poem, it comes as a 'given line,' and so it moves from the word. With the play, *La Corbière,* I think the work moved from both of these points together, but also from a passionate anger, that the real living women of the play had been treated as throwaway objects. I wrote to take them back from the sea, to bury them, to mourn them, to name them, to respect them. I wanted to redeem words such as 'whore,' 'harlot,' words of abuse, to give them back their own clean power, these words that are full of the sounds of the sea. I wanted to reclaim words such as 'cunt,' to place it close to 'love,' so that the women could make it their own and deny its insult. *La Corbière* happens on, in and through the sea and resounds with the music of wind, rock and stone.

Anne Le Marquand Hartigan, Dublin, 2001

www.ingramcontent.com/pod-product-compliance
Lightning Source LLC
Chambersburg PA
CBHW072105290426
44110CB00014B/1831